GREAT INVENTIONS
GUNPOWDER

STEWART ROSS

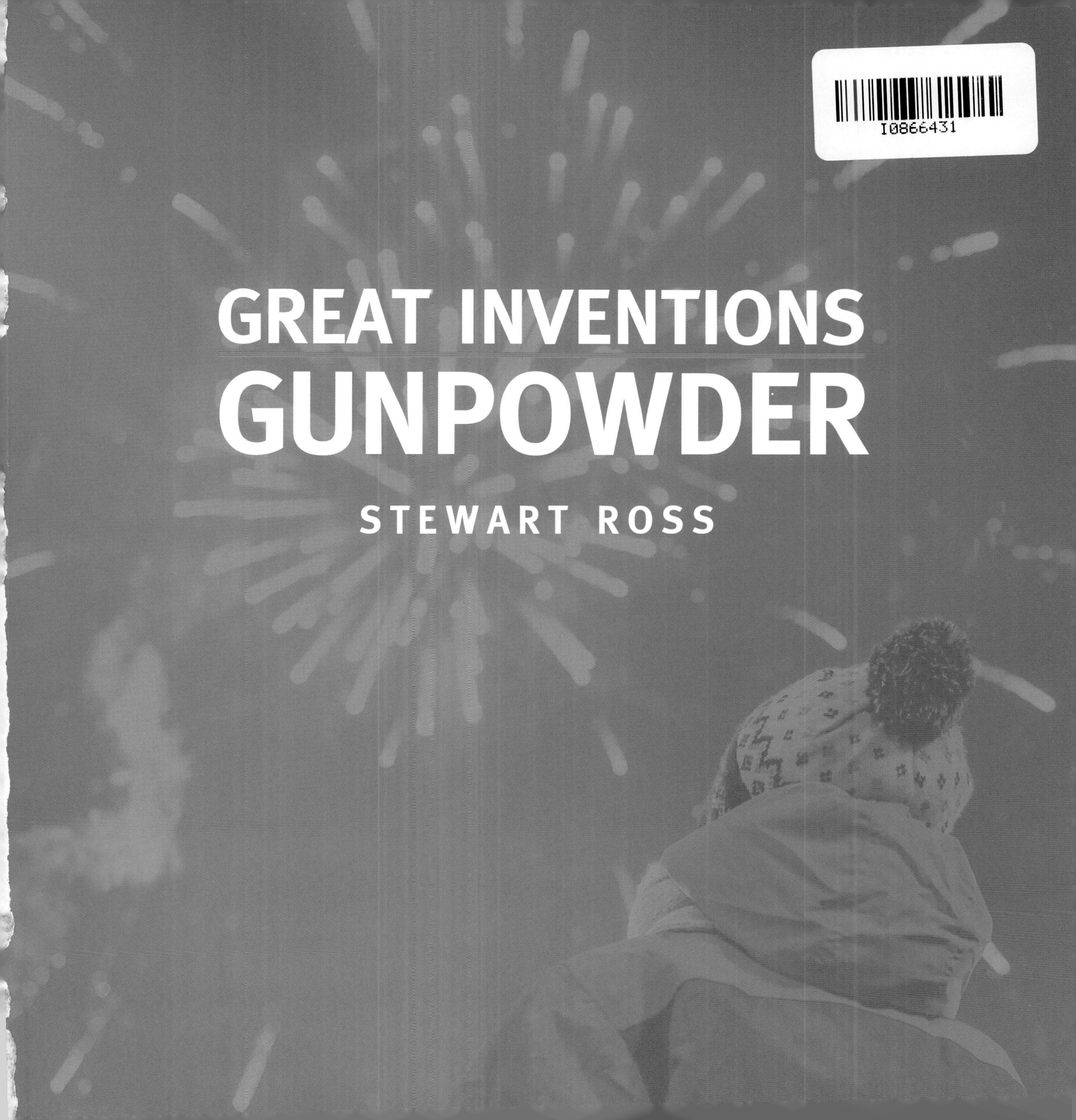

TULIP BOOKS®

Text by Stewart Ross

ISBN 978-1-78388-139-0

Index

Exploding medicine

Two thousand years ago, Chinese doctors made medicine from *saltpetre*. We call saltpetre **potassium nitrate**.

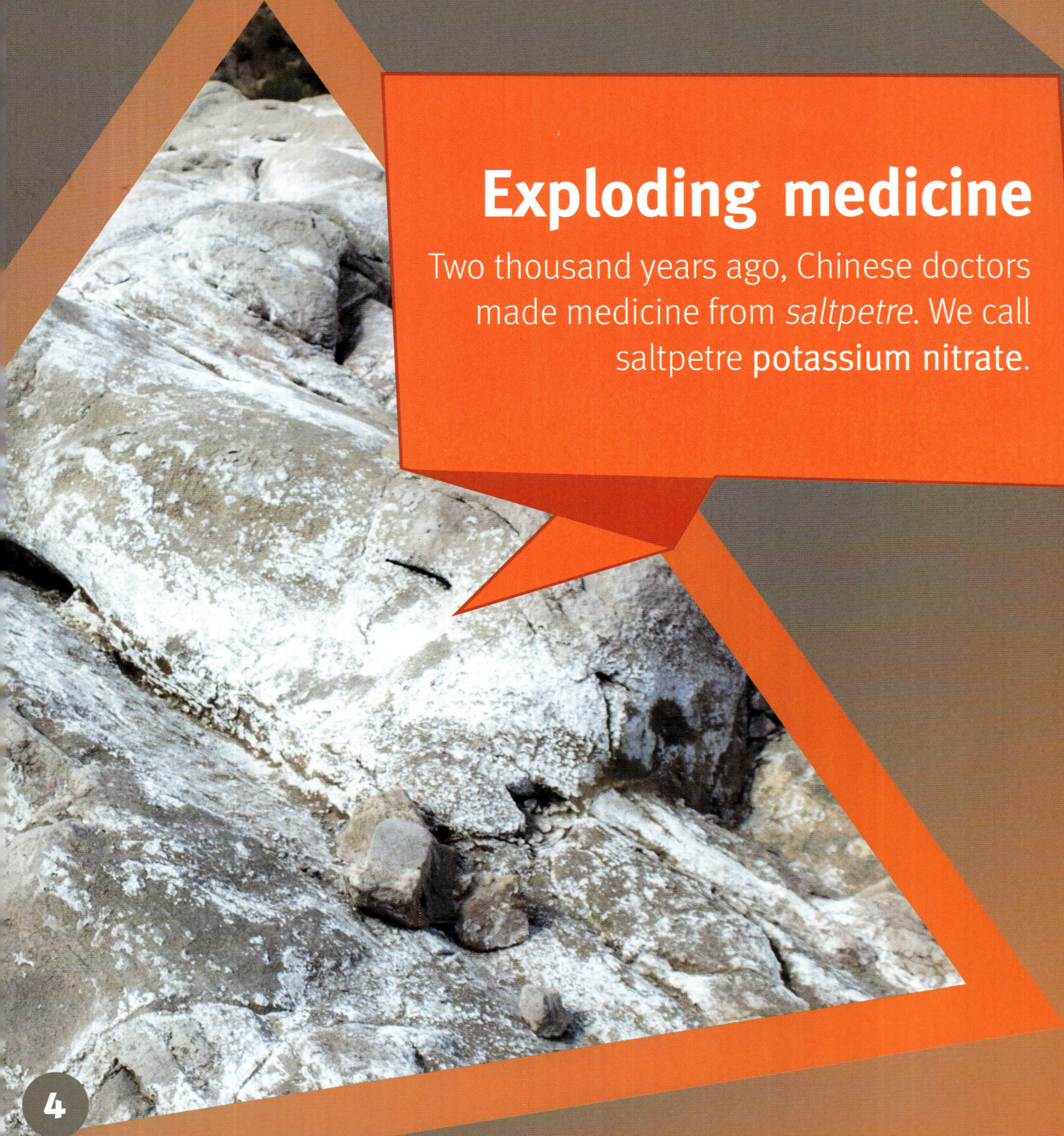

Later, the doctors mixed **saltpetre** with **charcoal** and sulphur. They wanted a new medicine. Instead, they had invented gunpowder!

WOW!

Potassium nitrate is added to cigarettes to make them burn evenly!

How does it work?

A gunpowder explosion is **very** quick burning (*combustion*). Combustion needs:

- Oxygen
- Fuel

In gunpowder, the oxygen comes from saltpetre, and charcoal is the fuel. Sulphur lets combustion happen at a low temperature.

I NEVER KNEW!

Gunpowder is 75% potassium nitrate, 15% charcoal and 10% sulphur.

Using explosions

Scientists set off gunpowder explosions in strong tubes. The explosions did two things:

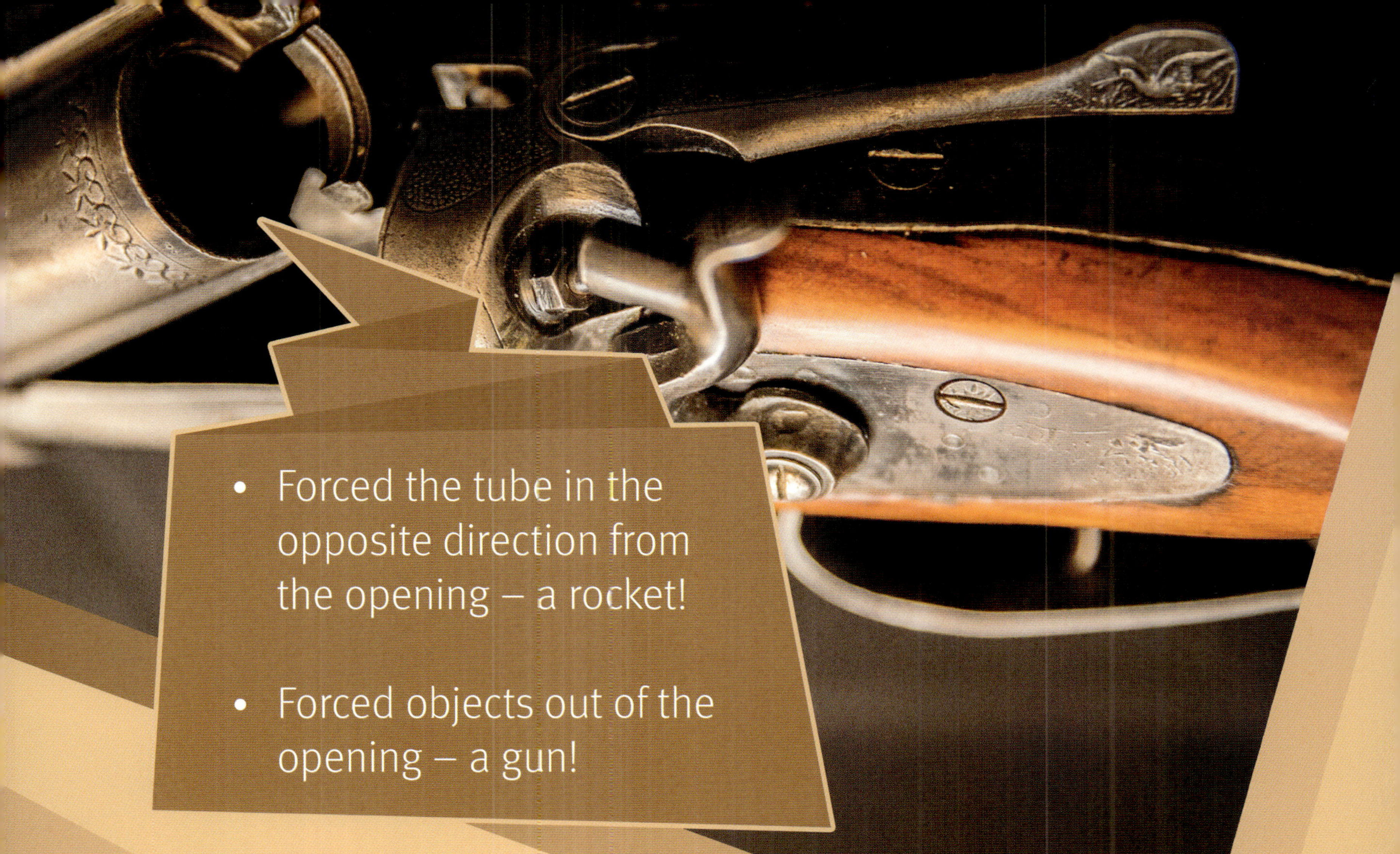

- Forced the tube in the opposite direction from the opening – a rocket!
- Forced objects out of the opening – a gun!

I NEVER KNEW!

Gunpowder is also known as black powder because it makes *black smoke* when it burns.

Early explosions

More than 1,000 years ago, Chinese soldiers began using gunpowder as a weapon. They made flaming fire arrows.

A few years later, they learned to shoot arrows out of gunpowder tubes.

WOW!

The first gunpowder was made of saltpetre, sulphur, charcoal – and honey!

Cannon

Gunpowder tubes made of metal could shoot out stones and bits of iron.

By about 1200 CE, the Chinese were making large gunpowder tubes for bombarding castles and towns. These were the first cannon.

WOW!

The cannon idea came from the *fire-lance* – an upside-down rocket on a stick that spat fire at the enemy!

Handguns

Gunpowder was used in smaller guns, such as the **arquebus**, **musket** and pistol.

The first handguns were heavy and slow to load. The gunpowder was lit by a match or a spark when **flint** hit steel.

I NEVER KNEW!

The first handguns did not have a trigger – they were really hand-cannons!

Rockets

Like guns, rockets spread to the West from China. Armies fired them against their enemies in battle.

Metal rockets were invented in India in the 18th century. These were bigger and had a much longer range.

I NEVER KNEW!

Rockets had peaceful uses, too – they carried ropes to sailors on sinking ships, for example.

Breech-loading

Early guns were *muzzle-loading*: gunpowder and shot were loaded down the barrel.

In the mid-19th century, breech-loading guns were invented: gunpowder and shot were loaded at the *back* end of the barrel. Much quicker!

I NEVER KNEW!

The invention of breech-loading led to the quick-firing machine gun.

High explosives

Gunpowder is not used much nowadays. High explosives, like **dynamite**, have replaced it.

WOW!

Alfred Nobel, who invented dynamite, called it Safety Blasting Powder. Actually, it wasn't safe – his brother was killed by an explosion in the dynamite factory.

The combustion of high explosives is much quicker than gunpowder. They are more powerful – and make a much louder bang!

Fireworks

Nowadays, gunpowder is used mainly in fireworks – another Chinese invention.

The colours in fireworks are made by adding tiny bits of metal to the gunpowder. Steel gives a yellow flame, for example.

I NEVER KNEW!

In Britain, 5 November is 'Firework Night'. It celebrates the discovery of a plot to blow up the government – with gunpowder!

Glossary

Arquebus
A large, early handgun, usually resting on a stand.

Breech-loading
Loading a gun by opening the closed or back end of the barrel.

Charcoal
Wood that has been heated but not burned.

Dynamite
A high-explosive made by mixing nitroglycerin with substances that make it more stable.

Flint
A hard, sharp stone.

Musket
An early type of rifle.

Oxygen
A colourless gas that is needed for combustion.

Potassium nitrate
A substance made up of potassium, nitrogen and oxygen.

Sulphur
A solid, yellow element that burns easily.

Trigger
The mechanism for firing a gun.